The Monster
in the
Wardrobe

PAUL SHIPTON

Illustrated by Chris Smedley

PACIFIC
L E A R N I N G

05 04 03 02 01
10 9 8 7 6 5 4 3 2 1

Published by
Pacific Learning
P.O. Box 2723
Huntington Beach, CA 92647-0723
www.pacificlearning.com

ISBN: 1-59055-032-3
PL-7404

Contents

1

Only for Real Monster Lovers

No doubt about it, I thought to myself: *My little brother is one weird kid.*

Here's why. I had to write a story for English class, but I couldn't think of a single idea. So Luke had given me one of his stories. It might give me an idea for a story of my own, he'd said.

The problem is, all of the stories he writes are about vampires and monsters and mummies and nice stuff like that.

Like the story I had
in my hands now – it
was called "Night of
the Flesh-Eating
Spiders."

I was up to the part where Brad
McSteel, the strong-jawed hero, was
trapped in the attic by an oversized
spider from another planet.

I sighed and read what Mr. Yokito,
Luke's teacher, had written at the end:

Poor Mr. Yokito! Imagine having to
read all of the crazy stories by my
monster-fanatic brother! No wonder
they say teachers have a hard job.

Just then there was a knock on my wall. It came from Luke's room and it was followed by a thin cry.

I threw the story down onto my bed and got up. I had a good idea what this would be about.

Sure enough, Luke was sitting up in bed. He had the covers pulled right up to his chin. The light was off, but the hall light was on, so I could still see into his room. Luke's monster posters looked creepy in the half-light.

"What is it?" I asked, already knowing what the answer would be.

Luke raised a shaky hand and pointed toward his old wardrobe.

There's a noise... I heard it.

His voice was as shaky as his hand.

Was it coming from in there?

He nodded. A few days ago, Luke had seen a movie about a monster that crept into kids' bedrooms. It lurked behind closed doors and waited until the dead of night to pounce. Sure enough, Luke was now imagining that *he* could hear mysterious noises in his room at night.

On nights when Mom was home, Luke would call for her when he got scared. On nights like this, when Mom was working the night shift at the hospital – she's a doctor – Luke usually called me.

(Dad was home, but he wasn't very sympathetic. He just kept trying to convince Luke that the monsters were "all in his head.")

I walked over to the wardrobe and pulled the door open. I gasped.

I smiled at him. Like I told you, my little brother is weird. Still, you can't help feeling a little bit sorry for him. He just has an overactive imagination, that's all.

"Listen, Luke," I told him. "There's *nothing* hiding in the wardrobe. This is an old house, and old houses make a lot of noises – floorboards creaking and stuff like that. That's all."

I sat on his bed.

Why don't you keep the light on and read for a little while? That always helps me get to sleep.

Luke nodded and grabbed a book from his shelf.

"How about this one?" he said. "I got it at a yard sale with Mom this afternoon."

He waved the book proudly.

My first thought was that he'd been robbed. The book looked like it was about to fall apart. Then I glanced at the title: *Big Book of Monsters.*

There was no picture on the cover, but there was a sticker that said:

**Warning: Only for Real
Monster Lovers.**

"That's not quite what I had in mind," I said. "Don't you have anything else?"

Luke stared at me blankly. I looked at his shelf stacked high with horror and science-fiction books and told myself not to ask silly questions.

Well, okay – but don't read for too long. Good night.

2

The Wardrobe Opens

Back in my own room, I wondered
why so many kids were crazy about
monsters. I mean, Luke was nuts about
them, but he wasn't alone in his
craziness. Lots of his friends shared his
strange interest in scary books and
comics. And I bet that, like Luke, they
ended up scaring themselves over
nothing.

I didn't understand it. Why like
something that makes you afraid?

Weren't there enough *real* things in the world to get scared about? Like whether you'd get a spot on the basketball team. *Or* whether you could get your homework done on time.

Speaking of which… I picked up a pen and waited for the perfect story idea to come to me.

I was still waiting and staring at a blank sheet of paper when the noise came again.

This time Luke was pale with fear. He stared at me with wide eyes.

What is it now? Don't tell me it's noises from the wardrobe again.

I was annoyed now. It was late, and I hadn't even *started* my homework.

Luke shook his head nervously and pushed the book toward me. I glanced down at the open page.

The Monster in the Wardrobe

One of the most terrible monsters of all, this unstoppable beast only comes out to feed at night. It prefers to eat young humans, though it'll make do with adults if there's nothing else available. Able to see in the dark, it

I had read enough.

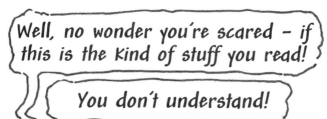

He pointed to the picture in the book. It showed a gruesome monster with a mouth full of jagged teeth.

The monster in the wardrobe.

That monster needs a good dentist, I thought to myself. I wanted to laugh, but Luke seemed really scared.

He stared at me. "That picture... It's *my* monster. The one I can hear in my wardrobe. The one I have nightmares about... I don't understand how, but it's there in the book."

I forced myself not to smile. I could see that he really believed all this garbage, and I didn't want to hurt his feelings. (I have to admit – I *can* be a pretty good big sister.)

So I thought carefully about what to say. I was still thinking when I heard the noise.

It was just a quiet scraping sound at first. It was coming from somewhere in the room, near the end of the bed.

It was coming from the wardrobe.

A sudden chill gripped me. What if Luke was telling the truth? What if there really was...? I shook the thought from my head and told myself not to be so silly.

Then the noise came again, only louder this time. Luke was frozen in fear. My mind was racing. Maybe it was a mouse that had gotten into the house. Or maybe something had gone wrong with the water pipes, or...

The wardrobe door slowly began to creak open.

Then something began to come out of it.

As if in a dream, I watched as a long, curved, SHARP claw slowly appeared around the wardrobe door.

A terrified croak escaped from Luke, and my brain kicked into gear. I grabbed my brother by the wrist and yanked him out of bed.

RUN!

It seemed like the most sensible thing to do.

3
Attack!

We didn't wait to see the rest of the
thing that was in the wardrobe. There
was no need – the sight of that hideous
claw was more than enough. We ran for
our lives and charged down the stairs.

Luke was still holding his book. He
was clutching it as if it was going to
save him.

I didn't have a plan. I didn't have a single thought except to GET OUT OF THERE AS FAST AS POSSIBLE!

I flung open the family-room door to get Dad. The TV was on – for some reason, even in my terror, I noticed that it was my favorite show – but Dad was not in the room.

However, the room was not empty...

A giant hairy spider was bobbing up and down over the sofa.

When I say a *giant* spider, I don't mean one like you might see in the shower. I mean a GIANT SPIDER. Huge, enormous, gigantic. It was so big that its eyes were level with mine.

I heard a scream. Then I realized that it had come from me.

Luke and I ran back into the hall. A cry of rage followed us from the family room. It was the spider!

My brain didn't have time to wonder why there was a giant spider in our house. It was too busy trying to keep me safe!

If we could just make it to the front door...

Another enormous spider sprang out in front of us. Another set of eight hairy legs began to edge toward us. We were trapped!

Without thinking, I grabbed one of Dad's golf clubs from the hall closet. I held it in front of me like a sword. The spider didn't stop moving toward me, but it slowed down.

Then it let out a terrible hiss and charged. I reacted quickly (I'm an excellent softball player – my reactions are good). I whacked the creature right on the head. It leaped back in pain.

The first spider had now followed us into the hall.

I jabbed at it, and this one stepped back too. I poked again, but it grabbed the club with its jaws. It was strong, and it almost managed to pull the club away from me.

My heart thudded in terror, but after a few long seconds I yanked the club free.

Luke, we've got to find a way out! I can't hold the two of them off much longer!

My brother wasn't listening. He was digging frantically in the dresser behind him. At last, he pulled out what he was looking for – a water pistol!

With trembling hands he filled the pistol with water from the vase of flowers on the dresser. I wondered what on earth he was doing as I gave each of the spiders another whack. My arms were beginning to ache.

Luke held the water pistol out at arm's length and pointed it straight at one of the spiders. At that moment, my skinny little brother looked like one of those heroes he was always reading about in his comic books.

He squirted water at the spider. As soon as it hit, the creature let out a shriek of agony.

There was a sizzling noise, and clouds of foul-smelling smoke began to billow from the spider. The hall was filled with the most disgusting smell.

Within seconds the creature had dissolved to a pile of dust.

Great!

Well, what else could I say?

The other spider bobbled nervously now and backed away down the hall. Luke stepped forward. I sensed a new confidence in my brother as he raised the water pistol.

He grinned as he pulled the trigger and... nothing. I followed Luke's horrified eyes down to the water pistol in his hand – it was empty!

Let's get out of here!

But how? We could hear the *clump, clump* of footsteps on the stairs. Somehow this did not sound like the spiders' skittering legs. These steps sounded heavier, more threatening. It had to be the monster from the wardrobe!

We were trapped – the spider one way, the monster the other way. There was only one place to go.

Quick! The basement!

4

The Monster Strikes

Luke's book was lying next to the
dresser. He'd dropped it when he was
looking for the water pistol. I don't
know why, but something told me to
grab it now.

"Come on!" screamed Luke. He and I
raced for the basement.

We tugged open the basement door.
As soon as we were inside, I checked the
lock. Then I checked it again. I had to
be sure.

We ran down the steps.

In the dim light of the basement's
single lightbulb, Luke and I looked at
one another. Each of us knew what the
other was thinking: we were trapped
down there. There was only one way in
and one way out.

My heart was beating wildly. I forced myself to take a deep breath, and then I looked around for something else to use as a weapon.

There was an old exercise bike nobody ever used and some boxes of our old toys and outgrown clothes. There was nothing else we could use. I tightened my grip on the golf club.

A question made its way through the panic in my mind.

An expression of disbelief mingled with the terror on Luke's face. He said slowly, "I knew because that's what happened in the story I wrote, 'Night of the Flesh-Eating Spiders.'"

Of course, Luke's silly story about giant spiders from outer space! But how?

That's when I remembered what Luke had said about his book. His own, personal monster – the monster in the wardrobe – had been in that book. Could the spiders be in there too? I flipped through the tattered book.

I slammed the book shut as if one of the spiders could leap off the page.

Then I looked at the cover. The warning sticker had begun to peel off, so I pulled it away. The full title of the book could be seen now. Both Luke and I gasped when we read it: *Luke McGuire's Big Book of Monsters.*

How could my brother's name be on the cover? A chill did sprints up and down my spine.

> **What's going on? Where did you say you got this book?**

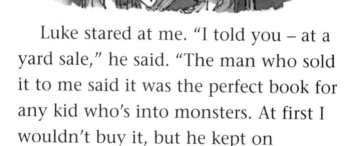

Luke stared at me. "I told you – at a yard sale," he said. "The man who sold it to me said it was the perfect book for any kid who's into monsters. At first I wouldn't buy it, but he kept on dropping the price."

I was baffled. This book was filled with all of the monsters from Luke's weird imagination... and somehow it was bringing them to life. But WHY?

I didn't have long to think the question over. Something hit the basement door with a heavy thud.

BOOM! Then again, and again.

I shook my head. This was something much bigger.

It had to be the thing from Luke's wardrobe.

With the next thud came a different sound – the crunch of splintering wood. The door was breaking! The monster from the wardrobe was about to get in!

5

Unstoppable!

What could we do? Panic clutched at my heart.

There was a sound of shattering wood and bending hinges. The door was history. A scream tore from Luke's mouth. A huge figure filled the open door frame.

I got a glimpse of a snout as long as a crocodile's. Deadly teeth flashed – lots of them. A clawed hand reached for the light switch.

Then the light went out and everything was pitch-black. I could feel Luke huddling next to me.

A heavy footstep sounded as the monster slowly began to come down the stairs. *Thud.*

It was followed by a scraping sound as clawed feet dragged across the concrete steps. Then again – *thud, scrape.*

My mind raced. Think! What did the book say about this thing? The word came back to me like a splash of cold water – *unstoppable*. Whatever you did, this monster would get you in the end.

Somehow Luke's book was the key to all of this. I frantically began to rip out pages and scrunch them up.

I didn't know if it would work, but I didn't have any other ideas.

The beast was almost at the bottom of the stairs.

In the darkness it was impossible to see what page I was tearing out. I just kept on ripping. Sooner or later I'd get the page with the monster in the wardrobe. I HAD to!

A soft chuckle sounded as the monster reached the basement floor.

We were doomed! Luke scooted back as far as he could. I went on tearing up the book and throwing away the pages.

Even in the darkness I could see a bulky shape loom in front of us. A pair of yellow eyes glowed menacingly in the blackness.

Then – *rip!* – I pulled out one more page and there was a sudden flash of light in the basement.

The monster was surrounded by swirls of light. It let out a low, puzzled grunt. Then the creature simply faded and disappeared. Soon all that was left was a pattern of stars dancing in the air.

Then there was nothing at all.

Luke's hand gripped my arm. I heard his voice in the darkness.

Before we did anything else, I ripped up the rest of the book. Whatever power it had, I wanted to make sure every bit of it was gone.

Then we nervously made our way up the stairs. We hardly dared to believe that it was all over.

I half-expected something to jump out at me. Nothing did. The place was a mess after our battle with the spiders, but the house was quiet.

We found Dad lying in the kitchen. He was asleep, and I could see wisps of silky thread around him. I guessed that one of the spiders must have wrapped him up and dragged him in there.

His eyes blinked open when we shook him. He looked pale, but he was unhurt.

I started to answer, but then I stopped myself. Where would I begin? I turned to my dazed-looking brother.

The Riddle of the Books

It was the middle of the night, but lights still blazed at the Darkwood Book Company.

In his office, Mr. Darkwood gently put down the phone. It wasn't good news. The book he'd sold to that boy, Luke McGuire, had been destroyed.

Darkwood stood and looked out into the night. Slowly he reached up and peeled the human mask from his face. That felt much better. To get things done, it was sometimes necessary to look like a human, but it always felt good to take off the mask.

Oh well. You win some, you lose some.

He had not won tonight – but he knew there would be other chances.

Anyway, things were going very well. Back in the old days, he had had to visit kids one by one. It had been fun, but it wasn't the best way for a monster to carry out its task of spreading fear across the land.

Even monsters have to change with the times. So Darkwood had come up with this new idea of using the books. Now, he could do his work much more quickly. He could scare hundreds of kids at the same time.

There was a timid knock at the door.
One of his workers came into the office.

The new books are almost ready, sir.

Darkwood smiled.

Very good. Now we just have to decide one thing – whose names will we use this time...?

About the Author

When I was growing up, I always wanted to be an astronaut, a professional soccer player, or (if those didn't work out for any reason) maybe a rock star. So it came as something of a shock when I became first a teacher and then an editor of educational books.

I have lived all over England and in Istanbul, Turkey. I'm still on the run and now live in Chicago, Illinois, with my wife and family.

Years ago, my monster lurked in the hall outside my bedroom. It never got me, and sometimes I still wonder where it went.

Paul Shipton